MW01122088

57 WAYS TO GROW YOUR BUSINESS

Bright Ideas for the Serious Entrepreneur

Better Numbers for Lawyers,

a division of Concierge CPAs, Inc.

8221 Brecksville Road, Suite 205

Brecksville, OH 44141

T: 216-333-3413

info@betternumbersforlawyers.com

betternumbersforlawyers.com

57 WAYS TO GROW YOUR BUSINESS

Bright Ideas for the Serious Entrepreneur

1   THE FOUR BASICS

All the ideas in this book ultimately revolve around four basic insights about growing a business. You can:

1. Increase the number of customers;
2. Increase the number of times each one does business with you;
3. Increase the average value of each transaction; and/or
4. Increase your own effectiveness and efficiency.

Here are some other business principles that we will explore later in the book:

> *"There is only one boss: the customer*. And he can fire everybody in the company, from the chairman on down, simply by spending his money somewhere else."*
> -Sam Walton,
>   Founder, Wal-Mart

- What you can measure you can manage.
- Build in unique core differentiators and focus on them constantly – it's more important to be different than it is to be better.
- Cutting the price is always an option but there is usually a better way – increasing value.
- Break compromises and lower the barriers to people doing business with you.
- Systemize every aspect of your business.
- Empower your team to make it right for every customer.
- Create a clear and detailed action plan.

* We have chosen to use the term **customer** throughout the book, while recognizing that many professional businesses may prefer the term **client**. We use the terms synonymously.

2   WHAT MATTERS TO YOU REALLY MATTERS

You own your own business for a number of reasons – these no doubt include:
- Providing for your family
- Being your own boss
- Making money
- Having flexibility
- Building equity

To help identify what really matters to <u>you</u>, complete the following questionnaire:

On a scale of 1 to 10 (where 10 is very important), how important are the following to <u>you</u>?

Issue	Importance
1. Increasing sales to existing customers	
2. Getting new customers we really want	
3. Expanding our range of products and services	
4. Improving quality and service	
5. Reducing our costs	
6. Energizing our team members	
7. Having a written strategic plan	
8. Having a detailed budget	
9. Getting accurate and regular reporting of budget to actual	
10. Knowing and tracking our KPI's	
11. Knowing how we're doing compared to others in our industry	
12. Improving cash management	
13. Reducing debt	
14. Having a succession plan or exit strategy	

15. Using new technology to improve productivity	
16. Having everyone follow uniform systems for all processes	
17. Having greater flexibility with work hours	
18. Taking more time off	
19. Funding my retirement	
20. Protecting my family against my death or disability	
21. Funding my children's education	
22. Protecting my business with funded cross-purchase agreements	
23. Building my personal wealth	

3   DO A SWOT ANALYSIS

As part of your business planning process, conduct a SWOT analysis to help you identify your company's
- Strengths
- Weaknesses
- Opportunities, and
- Threats

Here are some questions to ask:

Strengths
What are we really good at?
What are our unique competencies?
Where do we beat our competitors?

Weaknesses
What are we really poor at?
What resources are we short of?
Where are we at a competitive disadvantage?

Opportunities
How could we improve our sales?
How could we improve our efficiency?
What new products/services/niche markets could be added?

Threats
What regulations are changing?
What products/services are losing demand?
What resources are difficult to find?
What are our competitors doing?

A useful tool for deciding how to 'position' your products and services is the <u>Porter Generic Strategy Model</u> (developed by Michael Porter, Harvard Business School Professor, consultant and author of numerous texts on strategy).

The model suggests that companies are most successful when they stick to one box on the matrix. Rolls Royce, for example, goes after a **niche market** with a high degree of **differentiation**. Walmart, on the other hand, goes after a **total market** using a **low price** strategy.

Where do you think these well-known companies belong on the matrix?

> Nordstrom
> Mercedes-Benz
> United Airlines
> Apple
> Hyundai
> Walmart
> Southwest Airlines
> Cheapflights.com
> ATT
> Tesla

	Low/Modest Price	Other Differentiation
Total Market Focus		
Niche Market Focus		

Now, indicate where your company currently is and where you want it to be.

Deciding which box you fit in (or wish to fit in) will help you write your business plan, focus your marketing and define your Unique Selling Proposition (USP).

Here's another way to apply Porter's principles in your business:

First, make a list of the principal products and services that you offer. Then plot these on Grid A below:

Grid A

```
Easy        |              |              |
            |              |              |
            |              |              |
            |              |              |
Ease of     |              |              |
selling     |--------------+--------------|
each product|              |              |
            |              |              |
            |              |              |
            |              |              |
Difficult   |              |              |
           Low                          High
```

Expected demand for each product

Next, make a list of the principal industries, professions and types of customers that you serve. Plot each of these on Grid B below

Grid B

This exercise will tell you where to focus your marketing effort – namely in the upper right-hand quadrant of each grid (high growth and relatively easy). By focusing your energy on offering the right things – to the right groups – your marketing will be more successful.

5   DEFINE YOUR USP

Before you design your logo or write a clever slogan, you need to identify your Unique Selling Proposition (USP). This is your differentiator. This is what gives you an advantage over your competitors.

A winning USP:
- Makes a proposition to the customer that you will provide a specific benefit
- Includes a benefit that your competitors can't or don't offer
- Is a strong enough promise that it attracts customers

Examples of successful USPs include Apple's commitment to the most intuitive, sleekly designed technology, LensCrafters' focus on speed and convenience (or opening hours) and Southwest's focus on price ("We fly for peanuts").

Start by asking yourself and your team members to identify the following:
- The business you are in
- Your current and **desired** customers
- Your competition
- What makes you **different**
- The **unique** benefits that you offer your customers

Remember: "It's more important to be different than it is to be better."

Seth Godin wrote a wonderful book called <u>Purple Cow</u>.
This extract emphasizes the need to be different:
When my family and I were driving through France a few
years ago, we were enchanted by the hundreds of storybook
cows grazing on picturesque pastures right next to the
highway. For dozens of kilometers, we all gazed out the
window, marveling about how beautiful everything was.

Then, within twenty minutes, we started ignoring the cows;
the new cows were like the old cows, and what once was
amazing was now common. Worse than common, it was
boring.

Cows, after you've seen them for a while, are boring. They
may be perfect cows, attractive cows, cows with great
personalities, cows lit by beautiful light, but they're still
boring.
A Purple Cow, though. Now *that* would be interesting. (For a
while.)

Godin, S., <u>Purple Cow: Transform your Business by Being
Remarkable</u> (2003)

6 WRITE A BUSINESS PLAN

Planning is a key element in running a successful business. To get where you want to go, you'll need a business plan.

Most businesses don't have any kind of plan. So, start with a simple plan that pinpoints what you want to achieve. Here's an example:

1. In five years' time, I want the company to be worth $5 million
2. To achieve this, it must make annual profits of at least $1.5 million
3. To achieve this, it must have sales of $10 million
4. I need to increase my sales by, on average, $1 million a year
5. To do this, I will need to:
   a. Increase my customer base by 15%
   b. Increase the number of times my customers buy from me by 20%
   c. Raise prices by 10%

Having developed a basic plan, it's time to identify the constraints you think may get in the way of successful implementation:

1. INSIDE THE BUSINESS, WHAT ARE THE PRINCIPAL CONSTRAINTS ON OUR GROWTH?
   Some possibilities:
   - Lack of capital (financing)
   - Lack of credit from suppliers
   - Too many customers owe you money
   - Underperforming owners/attitude issues
   - Underperforming staff/attitude issues
   - Internal conflicts
   - Lack of direction
   - Outdated technology
   - Lack of marketing
   - Missing skills
   - Retirement and succession issues
   - Undesirable customers
   - Excessive payroll

- High occupancy costs
2. OUTSIDE THE BUSINESS, WHAT ARE THE PRINCIPAL CONSTRAINTS ON OUR GROWTH?

Some possibilities:

- The economy
- Regulations
- Competition
- Demographics
- Energy prices
- Freight costs

What you'll find is you can't do much about the outside constraints but you can do **a lot** about internal constraints.

Once you have a business plan, move on to setting targets for the short and medium term. Do this together with your team and make sure everyone understands the targets and how they will be achieved. Then make sure everyone agrees that they are achievable. If your team isn't willing to sign off that your targets are achievable, go back to the drawing board.

> Developing targets, forecasts and budgets can be a daunting task if you're not used to doing it regularly. As accountants, this is our "bread and butter" and we would be pleased to assist you.

Next, it's time to put together financial forecasts for the same periods. There's a temptation to do these just to satisfy some outside party such as a lender, but they are a key management tool. Highlighting deviations from forecasted numbers allows you to take corrective action more quickly. Your forecasts are dependent on assumptions and estimates and here's where it's important to be conservative. It's more fun to beat forecasts!

The last step in the process is putting together your near-term budgets, and here's where team input is critical.

Build budgets from the ground up; i.e. "here are our objectives, how much do you think we need to budget to achieve them?" rather than "here's your budget!"

8   TRACK YOUR KEY PERFORMANCE INDICATORS

Key Performance Indicators (KPIs) are the statistics you track to determine how well your business is doing. If you've been running your business for a long time you have developed your own KPIs, even if only on an informal basis. We think there's merit in formalizing your KPIs and setting up a system to measure and report them on a regular basis – many companies do it on a <u>daily</u> basis.

The first KPI we usually think of is net profit and its components: sales, cost of goods sold and operating expenses. While this information is certainly interesting, it's not much help in running the business. The information is historical and may not be available until long after the measurement period.

So let's look at some alternative KPIs:

<u>Sales</u> – we need to track sales constantly – in most enterprises, on a daily basis, with week-to-date, month-to-date and year-to-date information. The main value derives from comparing the numbers against budget and prior periods.

<u>Cash</u> – "Cash is King" as the saying goes, so you will want to track your cash balances, your accounts receivable and your collections. Likewise, you will want to keep track of your payables. Here's a simple format we have set up for several of our customers with a report generated at least once a week and preferably more often:

	Cash	Accounts Receivable	Accounts Payable
Start of day	$ 10,000	$ 100,000	$ 80,000
Sales		8,000	
Collections	5,000	(5,000)	
Purchases			4,000
Disbursements	(13,000)		(13,000)
End of the day	$ 2,000	$ 103,000	$ 71,000

Here are some KPIs that may be appropriate to your business – KPIs are generally specific to a particular business or industry:

1. Sales $ _____

2. # of Sales Transactions   _____

3. Average Sales Transaction $ _____

4. Cost of Goods Sold $ _____

5. Gross Margin %   _____

6. # of New Customers   _____

7. Average Sales per Team Member $ _____

8. Average Labor Costs per Team Member $ _____

9. Average Labor Costs as Percentage of Sales $ _____

10. Sales for Day of Week $ _____

Distribute your KPI information to everyone on the team. We call ours a "Flash Report" because it comes out "in a flash".

The above are "typical" KPIs for most businesses. What are some KPIs specific to your business and industry?

Specific KPIs to my business:

_____

_____

_____

_____

_____

_____

_____

_____

9   SYSTEMIZE EVERYTHING!

Theodore W. Garrison notes in his book The Magic of a Marketing System[1]:

> *Have you wondered how Ray Kroc managed to get teenagers in California, Illinois, Florida, and Maine to produce the exact same fry? It is really quite simple; McDonald's starts with the same kind of potato. Each potato is cut into fries of the same size. At all locations, the fries are cooked in the same type of oil in the same type of fryer at exactly the same temperature for exactly the same amount of time. Is there any surprise that all the fries come out the same?*

Just about everything that happens in a business is repetitive. That means that it probably doesn't have to be done by you! So here's a two-step approach:

1. Take a hard look at what you and your colleagues do each day and **write down** how it's done.
2. Start moving tasks to other people, by having them first observe how you do it and then doing it themselves with appropriate oversight.

Systemization is the key concept of The E-myth Revisited by Michael Gerber, one of the great guide books for entrepreneurs.

[1]As published in Marketing for People Not in Marketing – edited by Rick Crandall

10 APPLY THE LATEST TECHNOLOGY

Technology is a major driver of corporate profits. If you haven't already adopted these technologies, we would be pleased to discuss them with you:

1. Electronic document management
2. Electronic workflow
3. Multiple monitors
4. Portals
5. "Cloud" computing
6. Going paperless

There are major benefits to going paperless:

- Increase in productivity
- Elimination of storage space
- Reduction in expenses
- Ability to work remotely
- Better customer service
- Protection of documents
- Happier team members

There are also major benefits to being in the "Cloud":

- **Investment** – Cloud computing shifts a large portion of your IT costs from a capital outlay to a regular operating expense.
- **Expense** – Reduced IT expense as there's no need for expensive servers, hardware or IT departments.
- **Access** – Access your data from anywhere in the world with an internet connection.
- **Scalability** – Add users/programs/applications on an as-needed basis, allowing you to ramp up for a seasonal peak and then ramp back down again.
- **Speed** – Applications are infinitely quicker due to the capacity of the host's larger operating systems.
- **Security** – Data is backed up (in real time) and stored in multiple secure locations alongside Fortune 500 companies. The threat of having your servers stolen, subject to natural

catastrophe such as fire or flood, or being otherwise compromised, goes away.

11   OUTSOURCE

More and more companies are outsourcing various functions in order to focus on their core competencies.

Ask yourself these questions:
- What are we doing that is **not** our core competency?
- What do we do that we don't do well?
- What could we potentially outsource?

As an example, many companies have outsourced their entire accounting function to their accounting firm and have achieved significant savings.

This may be a good time for you to survey your customers – a project that should go well beyond just the issue of customer satisfaction. You want to understand your customers' real needs and wants, recognize areas that need improvement and identify new opportunities to expand your business. Some customers may be reluctant to give you their real, unbiased opinions if you conduct your own survey; so consider using a neutral party to conduct the survey for you.

Decide exactly what you want to find out before you launch the study and pre-test your questions as there are always some that are misunderstood or misinterpreted. You can also expect to receive responses or comments that you had not anticipated. Keep your survey brief and focused. Incentivize customers through a discount coupon (that can be used immediately) or offer a free gift or some other "freebie" and your response rate will be higher.

> One professional firm surveyed all 1,200 of their customers and received a phenomenal 50% response. How? The "freebies" were significant – in this case several iPads were given away.
>
> One of the partners did the drawing "on camera" and the firm posted the video on their website. Naturally, a link to this was sent to everyone who participated.

There are many ways to conduct your survey, including:
1. By mail (and include a postage paid reply envelope)
2. Over the web
3. By telephone
4. In person

Here's a sample cover letter:

Dear Customer:

We are here to provide high quality products and services to all of our customers. To help us achieve this, we would really appreciate your opinion on how we're doing. Please take a few minutes to complete the enclosed survey. Responses will help us identify where we're doing well and also where we need to improve.

Please return your completed survey in the enclosed self-addressed stamped envelope.

Thank-you in advance for your assistance. Please call me if you have any questions.

Sincerely,

Jane

If you are planning a telephone survey, hire someone to do this that has business experience, as much of the benefit comes from the answers to follow-on questions.

To achieve a high response rate, send the actual survey document in advance with a cover letter asking for the recipient's assistance.

Here's an example:

Dear Customer:

HOW ARE WE DOING?

We're anxious to find out! We have selected some of our favorite customers to participate in a survey.

We would <u>really</u> appreciate it if you could talk to our CPA, Andrew Amorov, when he calls. He is conducting the survey for us and will be calling you within the next ten days –- it should take no more than 8 – 10 minutes.

Thank you in advance for your assistance.

Sincerely,

Jane

P.S. I've attached a copy of the survey document Andrew will be using.

Here are 4 sample survey documents, from simple to complex:

<u>Satisfaction Survey – Sample A</u>

On a scale of 1-10, how willing would you be to recommend us to your friends, family and business associates? (10=very willing, 1=not willing)

<u>Satisfaction Survey – Sample B</u>

What do you like about our service?
What do you <u>not</u> like?
What can we do to serve you better?

Satisfaction Survey – Sample C

We would like to know how satisfied you are with the services and products we provide. Please rate each of the ten items listed below us on the following scale.

Extremely dissatisfied — 1
Slightly dissatisfied — 2
Neither satisfied nor dissatisfied — 3
Slightly satisfied — 4
Extremely satisfied — 5

How satisfied are you with:	
1. The location of our office (store)?	
2. The parking around our office (store)?	
3. Our scheduled office (store) hours?	
4. Our office (store) atmosphere and décor?	
5. The professionalism of our team members?	
6. The responsiveness and timeliness of our team?	
7. How your questions are answered?	
8. How you are treated on the phone?	
9. Our services and products?	
10. The prices/fees for our services and products?	

If you're doing a survey over the web, there are a number of popular systems available. A web survey will be your least expensive option; it will allow you to survey your customers more frequently (a good idea!).

Satisfaction Survey – Sample D

Listed below are the services and products we provide. For each one, please check the appropriate box 1 through 4.

Service or Product	1 We currently purchase this from you	2 We purchase this from another vendor	3 We do not use or need this	4 We do not currently use this but may need it
A				
B				
C				
D				
E				
F				

Checkmarks in columns 2 and 4 should spur you into action!

Once your survey has been completed, it is important to **do** something with the information, as a survey creates expectations among your respondents.

As a minimum, thank all the participants, with a letter such as this:

Dear Customer:

Thank-you for participating in our recent customer survey. We had an overwhelming response with many helpful comments and many, many excellent suggestions.

We will be working hard over the coming months to implement as many of these suggestions as we can.

Sincerely,

Jane

---

13 RESOLVE COMPLAINTS

If your customers have complaints that are appropriately resolved, they can become <u>better</u> customers than those who haven't complained.

Authorize your people to fix problems without any "run around" just as they do at Ritz Carlton Hotels. Give your people the authority to send a customer a bottle of wine, flowers, or whatever is appropriate – this becomes part of your company's "WOW" factor.

14   APPLY THE 80/20 RULE!

The 80/20 rule (also known as the Pareto Principle) says that 20% of your activities generate 80% of your results.

From this, we derive principles such as 20% of your customers generate 80% of your revenue. Do an analysis – group your customers together by "family" and related entities and see how closely this applies to your business.

Then it's time to assess whether you keep serving all of the 80% - you are probably <u>losing</u> money on many of them!

Here's an exercise to apply the Pareto Principle. It's called the Biggest Check Exercise. Here's how it works:
1. On the chart, list your 5 **best** customers (however you define that term).
2. In column A, enter the total revenue you generate annually from each customer and total the column.
3. In column B, enter the total revenue you <u>could</u> generate if you sold each customer your complete range of goods and services. Now total the column.
4. Compare the column A total with the column B total and ask yourself, "How should we change the allocation of our marketing and other resources?"

5 BEST CUSTOMERS	A	B
1.		
2.		
3.		
4.		
5.		
TOTAL		

Here's another exercise to help identify customers that should be fired:

Twice a year, get your whole team together and ask each person to nominate one, two or three customers for expulsion.

These "bad" customers tend to have certain common characteristics:
1. They are unprofitable or marginally profitable.
2. They argue about prices.
3. They are slow to pay.
4. They are high-risk.
5. They complain a lot.
6. They are slow to respond to requests.
7. They don't refer new customers.
8. They have unrealistic expectations.
9. They abuse team members.
10. They are rude, selfish or mean.

Once you've decided which customers need to go, you can decide on the best approach:
- Fire them in person,
- Fire them over the phone, or
- Fire them by letter or email.

If you decide to do it by letter or email, here's an example of suggested wording:

Dear John:

This letter is to advise you that due to changes in our practice, we will not be available to provide dental care to you and your family in the future and recommend that you engage another dentist. Upon your instruction, we will forward your dental records to your new professional.

Sincerely,

Joan

15   CONDUCT A FOCUS GROUP MEETING

Your business could probably benefit from convening a Focus Group.

Here's how it works:
1. Schedule a meeting at a desirable location, such as a restaurant or a hotel, with either lunch or dinner provided.
2. Contact a group of customers and ask for their help. Tell them that you would like to get their opinions and that this will be an opportunity to meet other successful business people.
3. Welcome your guests at the outset and introduce the facilitator, an experienced, neutral individual and then depart the scene.
4. Here are questions we want the facilitator to pose to the group:
   A. What does your business get right?
   B. What does your business get wrong?
   C. What could you do to produce a better overall customer experience?
   D. How do your best customers rate you on a scale of 1 to 10?

From the facilitator's report, you will gain insight into what your customers are **REALLY** thinking. Based on that information, you can build an even better business.

16   ANALYZE YOUR VALUE DIFFENTIAL!

Use the information you're gathering from your customers to establish (a) what they **value** and (b) what they **don't** value.

Here's how you do it. List all the key attributes of your products and services, such as:

1. Speed of delivery
2. Pricing policies
3. Range of products
4. Showroom
5. Website
6. Staff product knowledge
7. Staff responsiveness
8. Handling of complaints
9. Handling of product returns
10. Payment policy
11. Ordering system
12. Guarantees
13. Product catalog
14. Regular communications

Then ask your customers to tell you how important each of these attributes is to them on a scale of say, 1 – 10, with 10 being the most important and 1 the least. Next, ask your customers to tell you how they rate your company on these same attributes. From this information, you can develop a Value Differential for each attribute. Here's an example of what one might look like for a hotel:

Attribute	How important is this to you?	How do you rate this?	Value differential
1. Room Size	7	9	+2
2. Bed Quality	10	10	0
3. Furniture & amenities in rooms	5	10	+5
4. Friendliness	7	7	0
5. Hygiene	10	8	-2
6. Meeting Area	5	5	0
7. Architectural Aesthetics	5	9	+4
8. Late-open Restaurant/ Bar	10	2	-8
9. Room Service	10	10	0
10. Breakfast Quality	9	2	-7
11. Free Internet	10	0	-10
12. Child-friendly	0	0	0
13. Pet-friendly	0	0	0
14. Early check-in	10	5	-5
15. Free parking	5	10	+5
16. Automatic check-out	5	5	0
17. Coffee maker in room	10	0	-10

18. Price	7	8	+1
19. Refrigerator & Microwave in room	2	10	+8
20. Gift shop	5	5	0

In our example, number 10, "Breakfast Quality" is rated a 9 in importance and the hotel only gets a 2 rating, the value differential is -7.

Adding hot food and fresh fruit might be a smart move.

Number 11, "Free internet" is rated a 10 and the hotel gets a 0. It may be time to bundle this service into the room price as they do in some hotels.

Number 17, "Coffee maker in room" is rated very important, yet many hotels like this one do not provide one. It would be a relatively minor investment to satisfy customers.

The response to Number 19, "Refrigerator and Microwave", on the other hand, suggests that this is not a must-have item – therefore, an opportunity for savings.

From your own Value Differential Analysis, you may discover that there are areas where you are giving your customers either more or less than what they really want or care about.

Take a look at these options:
- A. Analyze your products and services and decide which must be offered as standard and which can be offered as options.
- B. Create a "naked" solution where all extras are optional.
- C. Introduce new products and services as options to see if they are valued.

17   GET YOUR PRICING RIGHT!

Many of us resist the idea of raising prices for fear that our customers will go elsewhere. We may think that price is the deciding factor behind most buying decisions. But this isn't true – buyers pay for a combination of value, service and convenience. So, raising prices may be an ideal strategy to improve your profitability.
Take a look at the following chart:

1.	**If your present profit margin is...**								
	20%	25%	30%	35%	40%	45%	50%	55%	60%
2.	And you increase your price by...								
	3. Your sales would have to fall by the following percentage before your profits decline...								
2%	9	7	6	5	5	4	4	4	3
4%	17	14	12	10	9	8	7	7	7
6%	23	19	17	15	13	12	11	10	9
8%	29	24	21	19	17	15	14	13	12
10%	33	29	25	22	20	18	17	15	14
12%	38	32	29	26	23	21	19	18	17
14%	41	36	32	29	26	24	22	20	19
16%	44	39	35	31	29	26	24	23	21
18%	47	42	38	34	31	29	26	25	23
20%	50	44	40	36	33	31	29	27	25
25%	56	50	45	42	38	36	33	31	29
30%	60	55	50	46	43	40	38	35	33

A Case Study

Elizabeth runs a bakery in a small town, offering a selection of breads, cakes and pies.

During her annual review meeting with her CPA, after the routine compliance issues were dealt with, they focused on pricing policies and how she marked up her bakery items. Elizabeth said "Well, I was intending to raise my prices next year, but there is another bakery in the area that is about 10% cheaper."

They then discussed the fact that she had a loyal customer base, had some special items that were not available at the other bakery and was always being complimented on the quality of her products.

Her CPA then showed Elizabeth the effect of a 10% increase in prices and the fact that she could afford to lose 22% of her sales volume and still make the same amount of money. They also looked at the other alternative of a 10% reduction in prices and how much extra volume she would need to generate to make the same amount of money. The result: she would have to sell 40% more baked goods to make the same profit as she was already making.

Here's what the analysis revealed:

Elizabeth's Bakery

	Last Year	As a % of Revenue
Sales	$ 293,842	100%
Direct Costs	190,932	65%
Gross Profit	**102,910**	**35%**
Expenses	26,138	9%
Depreciation	2,454	1%
Net Profit	**$74,318**	**25%**

Reduce expenses by	5%	Will increase profits by	$1,307
Increase sales by	5%	Will increase profits by	$5,146
Increase prices by	5%	Will increase profits by	$14,629
Increase prices by	10%	Will equal the same profit as before even if you <u>lose</u> volume of	22%
Decrease prices by	10%	Will equal the same profit <u>only if you</u> <u>increase</u> volume by	40%

What did happen in the next year? She put her prices up – bread by about 10%, and cakes and pies by about 20%.

Result – she made over $120,000!

18 BREAK SOME COMPROMISES!

Historical precedents within a particular industry force customers to make compromises or concessions.

Why, for example,

- Do most hotels not let you check in before 3 PM? [Hotel maids generally start work at 8 AM or 9 AM. Accordingly, there are made-up rooms available by mid-morning.]
- Are many stores catering to hobbyists closed on Sundays?
- Are most auto repair facilities closed on weekends?
- Is it so hard to buy a used car with confidence?
- Do supermarkets not provide childcare?
- Do retailers quote broad delivery times? ("We'll be at your house between 9 AM and 5 PM")

In your industry, what do customers have to put up with "just because"?

Think of the companies that have succeeded by breaking the "wait time" compromise, whether it's eyeglass manufacture ("in about an hour"), shoe repair ("while you wait"), movie ticketing ("print your own") or the punctual plumber ("paying you if they don't show up on time").

So break some of your own compromises, change your opening hours, offer a pick-up service or let customers pre-order over the internet.

19   OFFER MONEY-BACK GUARANTEES

Most companies offer an <u>implicit</u> guarantee of their products and some say "our products and services are guaranteed" – but that doesn't mean much. If you want your guarantee to make a difference, make it specific and credible. For example,

- If we don't show up within the time frame we promised, there will be no charge.
- You may return any item within 60 days of purchase.

Since your competitors may not offer such an explicit guarantee, it could be one of your key differentiators.

20   SURVEY YOUR COMPETITORS!

Most companies don't do this (believe it or not) but the information obtained can be really helpful in keeping you out in front.

1. Get your team together and complete a Competitor Worksheet on each of your competitors.
2. Obtain your competitors' brochures and promotional materials to find out what they think are their strengths and how they promote themselves. Look at trade journals and the web for product comparisons and reviews.
3. Collect other information by researching business data bases such as Dun & Bradstreet.
4. Meet with your customers and suppliers and ask them for their opinions on where you are better (or weaker) than your competitors.
5. Analyze the information and prepare spreadsheets showing comparative strengths and weaknesses.
6. Prepare an action plan!

Competitor Worksheet

Company name

Estimated annual sales

What are this competitor's most important strengths?

What are this competitor's most important weaknesses?

What do they do better than we do?

What do we do better than they do?

Who is this competitor's CEO?

What is their business approach/strategy?

What are the next strategic moves this competitor is likely to make?

What actions should we take to pre-empt or combat this?

21   SURVEY YOUR TEAM MEMBERS!

Your team members <u>should</u> know more about what's going on in your business than anyone else. Survey them regularly, and survey <u>all</u> of them.

Here's a suggested approach:
1. Prepare a questionnaire, allowing room for expansive answers.
2. Make it easy for people to respond (i.e. mail, email, fax etc.).
3. Make it voluntary and confidential.
4. Use an outside facilitator – this will help you get a higher response rate.
5. Insist (and publicize) that the outside facilitator maintains absolute secrecy as to individual responses.

Here's a sample questionnaire for team members:

<u>Data Gathering Questionnaire</u>

1. Identify at least three things that our Company does well and, in your opinion, should continue to do.
2. What are three things that our Company doesn't do well?
3. What have you heard from customers that concerns you the most?
4. If you were in charge, what are three things you would change immediately?
5. What opportunities should we be exploring?
6. How can we improve communications within our Company?
7. What things are people <u>not</u> talking about openly, but which should be addressed?
8. What causes you frustration about working here?
9. What do you believe are the key values of our Company?
10. What other suggestions do you have for the owners of the Company?

22   INCENTIVIZE YOUR TEAM!

Most incentive programs are sales-oriented because it is relatively straight forward to measure outcomes. Other incentive programs may be appropriate for such activities as personnel recruitment, cost containment or new ideas. Smart companies use incentives for their entire team to keep everyone focused and motivated.

Structure your incentives around whatever your team members find most rewarding. This may be cash, but merchandise, gift certificates or travel may be even more effective.

Set your incentives so they encourage teamwork – it's important that most people win. Make the time frame short enough so that team members can visualize the end result.

When working on goal-setting, remember the **SMART** acronym:
- **S**tretch
- **M**easurable
- **A**ttainable
- **R**elevant
- **T**imely

23   DEVELOP REFERRALS AND INTRODUCTIONS

Referrals are the lifeblood of a successful business – there's no better way of building sales than by increasing referrals. They are not only the #1 source of <u>new</u> business, they are the #1 source of the <u>best</u> new business.

People <u>like</u> to make referrals – when we make a wise purchasing decision, we want to share it with others as a way of validating our own good judgment and good fortune.

To get referrals, you have to ask for them! If you are talking to one of your customers you might say, "As you know, we do a lot of work with mid-sized companies like yours – showing them how to manage the cost of raw materials. If you know of anyone you think we can help, would you be willing to introduce us?" Almost every customer will say yes. Not all of them will follow through – but you've planted the seed!

> ### Stimulating Introductions
>
> At the end of each month ask yourself these four questions:
>
> 1. Are all my customers happy?
> 2. Have I given all my customers enough TLC (tender loving care)?
> 3. Have I talked to each of my customers?
> 4. Have I asked each of my customers for an introduction?

<u>Step 1</u> is getting people to agree to recommend you.

<u>Step 2</u> is making sure they have the materials needed to facilitate the process. Give them copies of your firm brochures, newsletters and specialty booklets. When you do, include a note thanking them for their help. Then, follow up with periodic letters and new marketing materials. In addition, make sure **everyone** in your organization carries business cards and that you have a great website.

Here are five strategies for developing more and better referrals (you may prefer the term introductions – it sounds more professional and less intimidating):

1. Provide your customers with a "WOW" experience.

2. Let your customers know up front that you will be asking for introductions. Explain how your business depends on positive word-of-mouth and specific recommendations.

3. When asking for introductions, be sensitive to timing. It takes practice and experience to do it effectively. The best time to ask, naturally, is when you have just completed a project or assignment. Ask for a testimonial letter – one that he or she would feel comfortable having you send to new contacts. Also, ask your customers to provide a review of your firm on review websites (such as yelp.com). Today it is the search engine of choice for many individuals and many different businesses. If you've never used it, log on and put in the name of your company to see what people are saying about you!

> **NEVER USE THE "B" WORD!**
>
> Saying that you're "BUSY" is the quickest way to dry up referrals. Using the "B" word reinforces any reservations people may have about your level of service and discourages them from sending you more business. If you appear unable to handle the work you have now, why would anyone want to send you more? When you're asked "how are you doing? or "how's business?" the answer is "Business is great...and we're looking for more!"

4. Tell your customers exactly what you want them to do and describe the kinds of new customers you are looking for. Then discuss people they might know who meet these criteria. Your customer may offer to make a contact. Ask for a commitment, and let him or her know you will be in touch regarding the opportunity.

5. When you do receive a referral, make sure to say "thank you", whether or not the referral results in new business. Set up a system so that every referral is properly acknowledged.

6. When you get a new customer as a result of an introduction, find a special way of thanking your referral source. Send a bottle or perhaps even a case of wine, a bouquet of flowers or a plant. The most memorable thank-you's will be specific to the individual such as:
    *   Concert tickets to a favorite band or orchestra
    *   A gift certificate to a favorite store
    *   Dinner for 2 at a high-end restaurant
    *   A signed baseball (for a baseball fan)

There is no better way to build your business than through referrals. Like you, most business owners and professionals are looking for new business. If you want people to make referrals to you, find a way to do the same for them.

Here's a sample "Thank you" letter for a referral:

Dear Gail,

Thank you for referring Victoria DeYonge to our firm.

We always welcome new customers and when they are introduced by a valued individual like yourself, it makes it all the more special.

We met with Victoria this week and look forward to helping her.

Again, thank you for the introduction!

Sincerely,

Jose

Tip: This will be particularly effective if it is handwritten on a "Thank you" card. Enclose a Starbucks or an iTunes gift card to make your "thank you" special and different. Or use this as an opportunity to promote one of your customers, through a gift certificate. That way, everybody wins.

Believe it or not, customers make most of the major judgments about you and your company within the first few minutes of meeting you or your company's representative.

Dress

Team members should always be properly dressed – establish clear guidelines as to what is acceptable, even if your firm does not have a specific dress code. Customers have expectations as to how a representative of a particular business or profession should be dressed – this one factor is of disproportionate importance, as documented many years ago in <u>Dress for Success</u> (1988, Molloy, J., Warner Books). And remember, it's always easier to dress down than it is to dress up.

Enthusiasm

There's just no substitute for enthusiasm. A customer wants to know that you and your team are 100% committed to your products and services. Train your team members to say – when asked what they do – "I work for the best _____ in town/in the _____ industry. For example, "I work for the best consulting firm in the forest products industry."

Professionalism

This is achieved when members of your team demonstrate:
- Product and service knowledge
- Acceptance of responsibility
- Competence
- Dependability
- Responsiveness
- Active listening
- Keeping promises
- Diagnosis before prescription

Now may be a good time to do an overall "image audit" of your company. Here's a checklist:

Team member dress

Enthusiasm

Professionalism

Business cards (everyone should have one)

Company branding

Physical appearance of the business

Product packaging

Stationery

Signs

Unique Selling Proposition (USP)

Be a Good Listener!

When you're meeting with a customer or prospective customer (particularly if you haven't met them before):

- Ask if it's OK to ask some questions
- Ask "open questions", i.e. those that require more than a yes/no answer
- Ask for clarification or elaboration of a customer's statement
- Ask if it's OK to take written notes – this tells the customer that what he/she is saying is important
- Don't interrupt
- Don't argue or contradict
- Repeat back the customer's goals, issues or concerns to reinforce and clarify

25 ANSWER THE PHONE!

Customers talk to your receptionist more often than anyone else in the company – yet most receptionists have less than ten minutes of training! Check with your phone company – most of them run training programs on receptionist skills. Ask friends to call your office and report back on their experience. Then have a company session to make sure everyone answers the phone in exactly the same way and in a super-friendly tone of voice. For example, "Good morning, Angel & Company, this is Carol. How may I help you?"

Call your office outside of office hours and listen to your recorded message. Is the message upbeat and friendly? Is it consistent with your company's values? Is it current and up-to-date?

Some firms pay their receptionist a bonus for each new customer appointment, just to emphasize the importance of how the phone is answered when someone calls your company.

26 MAKE YOUR RECEPTION AREA SPECIAL

Your reception area communicates the image that you want to project, so let's make it special!

Here are three ideas:

Idea #1
Create a slideshow!
Install a plasma screen in your reception area and run a 5-10 minute PowerPoint slideshow. This gives you an opportunity to make people aware of your complete range of products and services.

Idea #2
Create a menu!
Instead of the typical "Can I get you a cup of coffee?" let's be different. Present your customers with a menu of available drinks, and if you **are** serving coffee, be sure it's the best – there's nothing like a "proper" cup of coffee.

And how about installing a cookie maker in the office kitchen? Offering fresh-baked cookies to your visitors should keep everyone in a positive frame of mind.

Idea #3
Create a theme!
When you're deciding what to put on the walls of your reception area, have a consistent theme. Anything unusual, particularly if it's related to the interests of the owners, will get people's attention.
- Framed photographs of what your street looked like 100+ years ago – readily available from your local Historical Society
- A collection of baseball caps
- A selection of paintings by one of your customers
- Pictures of your Company's owners as children, members of the military, or doing their favorite recreational activity

Your reception area may be the only part of your business that a visitor sees, so make it **interesting** and **different**.

27   HIRE A MARKETING PERSON

Implementing an effective marketing program involves a substantial amount of effort, but as we shall see in succeeding chapters, much of the work is repetitive and can be systemized.

You need someone to coordinate your marketing activities who doesn't have a bunch of other responsibilities that will get in the way. This person can be either full-time or part-time and could be anyone from a student intern to a highly experienced professional. Initially, ask them to update the contact management database and launch a direct mail program – making sure that all marketing correspondence and required phone follow-up gets done on a timely basis.

Marketing people may have different titles depending on their level of experience, responsibility and compensation:
- Marketing assistant
- Marketing coordinator
- Marketing manager
- Marketing director

> **Marketing is for Everyone!**
> Receptionists and other front-line personnel usually have more contact with customers than do more senior people. When we fly, we have more contact with the skycap than we will ever have with the pilot.
>
> Expect and encourage **everyone** to be a marketer. Everyone – from the receptionist to the CEO – is there to provide a "WOW" experience for each and every customer.

Here are attributes to look for in a marketing person:
- Excellent social and verbal skills
- Good written communications
- Computer and database experience
- Event organizing skills
- Attitude and enthusiasm (the most important!)

Here is a sample list of responsibilities for a marketing person:

1. Mailing list maintenance
2. Welcome letters to new customers
3. Welcome gifts to new customers
4. Holiday and birthday cards
5. Year-end gifts to customers and referral sources
6. Year-end thank-you letters
7. Direct mail
8. Phone follow-up
9. Production and distribution of company brochure
10. Production of booklets, catalogs and specification sheets
11. Production of help sheets
12. Newsletters
13. Customer satisfaction surveys
14. Follow-up on customer satisfaction surveys
15. Lunch program organization and follow-up
16. Company party or open house
17. Speaking opportunities
18. Press releases
19. Conference room use by customers and non-profit groups
20. Seminars
21. Events
22. Web site
23. Advertising
24. Monitoring of individual marketing goals

There are two parts to having a recognizable brand identity, the first being a logo and the second being a tag line. Your logo is key to your company identity, so get one that is colorful and distinctive. Before you begin the process of logo design, do this exercise. List 10 adjectives that people now use about your company or about the people who work in your firm. Now list 10 adjectives that you would **like** people to use about you. Here's the result from a law firm that did this exercise:

Current Adjectives	**Desired Adjectives**
Conservative	Proactive
Accurate	Approachable
Forthright	Caring
Competent	Trustworthy
Thoughtful	Communicative
Expensive	Responsive
Diligent	Professional
Professional	Imaginative
Learned	Timely
Thorough	Consistent

Give the results of this exercise to the people designing your logo – it will point them in the right direction.

There are four common types of logos:
1. Your company's name in a distinctive type
2. Your company's initials
3. An abstract symbol
4. A realistic symbol

When considering a Company logo, here are some questions to ask:

1. Does it project who we are? Make sure it fits your company's values and personality.
2. Does it have movement? If you want to project the idea that you are innovative and proactive, then develop a logo that has movement (generally left to right).
3. Does it have color? People expect things to be colorful, so use a distinctive color for your logo, but make sure it works in black and white and in different sizes — your logo may appear in newspapers, magazines or other media, keep it simple and crisp.

The importance of a slogan or "tag line" is similar to that of a logo. It is one of the key ways you differentiate your company from others.

Try the exercise below to develop your slogan. Do it along with all your team members, so that you can reach a consensus that everyone supports.

TAG LINE EXERCISE

What are the 3 most important qualities that we want to convey about our company?

1. _____

2. _____

3. _____

Of these, which is the **single most important**?

Now, develop your slogan around this one idea.

Here are some examples:
- Business is great and we're looking for more!
- We start where other _____s finish
- On the Ball

- We care
- The Problem Solvers
- Your success is our bottom line
- _____s for Life
- Connecting the dots
- 24/7
- Our customers are family
- We change lives
- People. Ideas. Action.
- Trusted Advisors
- Vision
- Results not excuses

29   BUILD A CONTACT MANAGEMENT SYSTEM!

In this business environment, you need to collect and manage a lot of information about your customers, prospects and referral sources.

To do this, you need a robust Contact Management System, which will incorporate Customer Relationship Management (CRM). The system allows you to keep regular contact with selected customers, prospects and referral sources with a minimum of effort and it helps you manage the sales process. Popular programs include:
1. Microsoft Contact Manager
2. Salesforce.com
3. ACT!
4. Goldmine
5. Maximizer
6. Zoho.com

In addition to the obvious function of maintaining names and addresses of companies, contacts within those companies and other individuals, contact management programs have numerous additional capabilities, such as:
- Ability to tag each name with **multiple attributes** such as customer type, industry, profession, specialty, size of business, size of town, number of employees, birthday, anniversary date, SIC code, and responsible individual.
- Ability to sort and create lists by **multiple attributes**. For example, your contact management program could quickly identify everyone in the database who
  - is a real estate agent, and
  - is in a particular city, **and**
  - has a specialty in commercial property.
- Ability to do direct mail **without mail merging** from another program, since your contact management system has its own word processing system.

- A reminder system that tells you, among other things, when to follow-up on a mail piece – this feature is **essential for telemarketing**.
- Ability to **import mailing lists** in various formats.
- A note-taking function where you can **summarize conversations** with a contact. You can also "attach" documents to a name.
- Email via **Outlook** directly from the database.
- Links to popular software packages such as Excel and QuickBooks.

Many contact management programs also have popular features such as:

- Scheduling
- Phone Logs
- Call reports
- Personal calendars
- To-do lists
- Expense reporting
- Automatic dialing
- Customer recognition on inbound calls
- Automatic email capture
- Sales pipeline management

Customer Recognition

Make everyone in your office responsible for being a "clipping service." Ask them to clip out anything they see in a newspaper or other publication relating to a customer or friend of the company.

Also, sign up for Google Alerts and socialmention.com with all your customers' names. Whenever a name shows up, you'll get an alert. And when they are mentioned – shoot them a congratulatory email (assuming it's positive).

In addition to tracking your customers on Google Alerts, put in your company name and the names of all your team members.

Could be interesting!

30 BUILD A HELP SHEET SYSTEM!

Many of your customers will face similar business challenges, so develop a Help Sheet System. Here's how it works:

- Write one-page white papers (or "help sheets") on nine separate topics which are of interest to customers.
- While a customer is waiting to see you, have your receptionist hand him/her a clipboard with a list of the help sheets and a request to "please check off the ones you'd like and I'll print them out for you."
- The receptionist then puts together a promotional pack, including the selected help sheets, and brings it to you. You can then give it to your customer – this should lead to a broader conversation and additional opportunities.
- Be able to request them online.

Here is a suggested list of help sheets for an attorney's office:

1. Is your will up to date?
2. Do you have a living trust?
3. Does your business have a buy-sell agreement?
4. Forms of doing business – pros and cons.
5. Do you need an estate plan?
6. Education plans for children and grandchildren.
7. What's your business exit strategy?
8. Minimizing and managing risk.
9. Asset protection opportunities.

Here's a list of help sheets that might be appropriate for an electrician:

1. The importance of an annual safety check
2. Saving money on your utility bills
3. Keeping your home safe for children — A 10-point checklist
4. Surge protection and fire dangers
5. Fire alarm options
6. Electricity and water don't mix

31   CREATE A "FREEBIE" KIT!

So what's a "freebie" kit? Answer: something that a customer finds really useful and that you are happy to give away:

Here are some examples:

Computer Company. A Basic Systems Kit, explaining:
- Various systems
- How they are configured
- Avoiding problems
- Maintenance backup checklists.

This might also include a free disk with shareware and virus protection programs.

Insurance Broker. A kit explaining the different forms of insurance, what various terms mean, how to avoid claims and approaches to risk management.

Appliance Store. A catalog describing products, prices, warranties and maintenance tips.

Law firm. A booklet summarizing legal issues for small businesses, such as:
- Selecting a legal entity
- Incorporation (articles, bylaws, etc.)
- Buy/sell agreements
- Landlord/tenant issues
- Lease issues
- Product liability
- Employment law (hiring procedures, termination procedures, employment rights)

Once you've created your "freebie" kit, get it distributed. For example, the above law firm would make their "freebie" kit available to:
1. Existing customers
2. Prospective customers
3. Accountants
4. Bankers

5. Financial Advisors
6. Real Estate Agents
7. Insurance Agents

You will also be using your "freebie" kit as a key element of your direct mail program.

If you're producing a book or a kit, consider the print-on-demand services of Amazon. Go to createspace.com. You can print from 1 copy to 1,000 for a fraction of what it used to cost.

32 GATHER TESTIMONIALS!

What your customers say about you is infinitely more persuasive to a prospect than anything you could possibly say about yourself. Hence, the popularity of websites such as traveladvisor.com and yelp.com.

Many customers are pleased to provide a testimonial if you make it easy for them. When a customer compliments you on your product or service (usually at the point of delivery), respond accordingly:

> *"Thank you for your comments. We would really appreciate a written testimonial from you. May I draft something up for you to review and send back to us?"*

Then consider all the ways you can use these testimonial letters:

1. Put them on your website
2. Put copies in a binder and keep it in your reception area.
3. Make another binder to take with you when you go on sales calls.
4. Have the original testimonial letters individually framed – hang them throughout the office.
5. Include pictures of your customers – they will make the testimonial letters even more effective.

33 DEVELOP A BROCHURE

Basic marketing materials – often referred to as collateral materials – include a company brochure and, depending on your business, various booklets or specification sheets promoting your products, services or the industries that you serve. It's nice to have something <u>tangible</u> to give people – it helps establish credibility.

Here are some suggestions for preparing a brochure:

- Keep it simple – you may only need a few pages. Consider a bi-fold or tri-fold that can be easily mailed in a regular envelope or carried in a jacket or purse.

- Include testimonials from customers – they are infinitely more compelling than anything you could write about yourself.

- Cut the boiler plate information to a minimum. The key information a customer needs is:
  - Where are you located and how do I find you?
  - Where do I park?
  - How do I contact you?
  - What's your web address?

Now focus on what makes you <u>different</u>:
1. Benefits of selecting your company
2. Opening hours
3. Unlimited telephone support
4. Range of products/services
5. Timeliness of delivery
6. After-sales service
7. 24/7 support
8. Resource center
9. Free samples
10. Clear pricing structure

Things to minimize or avoid:

1. Overuse of words "we" or "our" – instead use the words "you" and "your."
2. History of the company
3. Features of the company
4. Pictures of all team members (one of them always seems to leave the day after the brochure has gone to print!)

Now that you have produced your brochure, develop a distribution plan:

1. Send two copies to all your customers and referral sources. Ask them to pass along the second copy.
2. Create a display in your reception area.
3. Keep a supply of brochures with you, and make sure your other team members do the same.
4. If you get the opportunity to make a speech, distribute your brochure to audience members beforehand (by putting a brochure on each chair, for instance). That way, they are familiar with you and your products or services before you start talking and will be more likely to focus on your message.
5. Include some marketing literature with each piece of correspondence you send out, both to customers and prospects.

A website and a general brochure may be all you need to promote your business. But if you specialize in serving specific industries or professions, you will want to have specialized booklets for each industry/profession you serve or each product or service you offer. They don't need to be expensive – they just need to be **specialized** and look professional.

One of the great advantages of technology is that it has leveled the playing field for smaller companies competing with larger ones. The internet gives you the ability to communicate regularly with all the people on your mailing list.

Send out a brief e-newsletter at least every 2 weeks. Make it short enough that someone can read it on screen without opening the entire document. Two paragraphs are usually sufficient. Focus on one issue only and provide enough information to generate a response from people who are interested in the subject. For example, you might answer a customer's question or describe a pending change in regulations.

> **Tip for Getting More Email Addresses**
>
> Wage a campaign to get all the email addresses of all of your customers, all of your prospects and anyone else in your database. Consider running a month-long competition – with prizes, of course – to see which of your team members can get the most email addresses.

Test email subject lines. One may get more opens than another. Always link to your website or blog to encourage more traffic. A **find out more information** link really helps. At the bottom of each e-newsletter, indicate how the reader can unsubscribe.

35 SEND PRINTED NEWSLETTERS

Newsletters are a great way to keep your name in front of your customers, prospects and referral sources. You might send a printed newsletter anywhere from one to four times a year to supplement your more regular email newsletters. Make your printed newsletter colorful, upbeat and readable. Here are some suggestions for content:

- A spotlight on one of your team members. People really enjoy human interest stories, such as marriages and promotions, and it's an opportunity to showcase your talent.
- An article about one of your customers. They will appreciate being featured and you can provide additional copies for them to send to **their** customers and prospects.
- A letter from you giving a success story and reminding readers that you are looking for more business.
- Attention grabbers such as cartoons, photographs, puzzles or recipes. One professional firm includes regular movie reviews — clearly not related to their services, but of immediate and universal appeal.
- A feature describing a recent speech you made, noting that you are always available to make presentations to groups.
- Some technical stuff may be good too!

Company news is appropriate, provided you are brief and stick to subjects that everyone can relate to, such as:

- New employees
- Births
- Engagements
- Marriages
- Awards

Good graphics are essential to maintain interest and the newsletter must be **interesting**. Your newsletter is an **entertainment** medium as well as an **educational** medium!

36   SEND WELCOME LETTERS!

This is a great way to cement relationships with new customers. It's an opportunity to:

- let new customers know how important they are;
- promote other products and services; and
- ask for referrals.

Your welcome letter might include:

- A warm welcome to the firm
- Contact information
- A request for referrals
- 2 business cards
- Your Firm brochure

Set up a system to send welcome letters **automatically**. You only get one chance to make a first impression, so don't omit this simple step. Make it a step in your new customer setup process so it never gets overlooked.

Here's an example:

Dear _____:

All of us at Janes & Company are delighted that you have selected us to help you. We pledge to provide you with the very best services and we look forward to a long and mutually rewarding relationship.

We are particularly pleased that you were referred to us by Jane Tang at Wells Fargo Bank. As a service business, we are dependent on referrals from our satisfied customers and good friends of the firm.

It is my responsibility to ensure that we provide world-class services. If you ever have a concern or wish to comment on our services in any way, please do not hesitate to call me. If you know of anyone else who might benefit from our services, please ask them to call – we are always looking for great customers like you.

Sincerely,

James Paterson

President

37 SAY THANK YOU!

Being successful in business is about relationships, and an effective way to maintain long-term relationships is through regular thank-you letters.

Email has taken over most interpersonal correspondence, so there's something special about receiving a personalized card or letter by "snail mail". Many successful entrepreneurs send several cards a day, customized with the company's logo, as an efficient way of staying in touch with customers, vendors and other contacts. Encourage your associates to do the same – perhaps even make it company policy!

TIP: When you are sending a welcome letter or a thank-you letter to one of your customers, include at least 2 business cards and a brochure, if you have one. Make it easy for people to refer you to new prospects!

Here's an example of a great thank-you letter:

Thank you! Thank you! Thank you!

Sometimes we just don't say "thank you" often enough. I want you to know that we **really** appreciate your business and your referrals.

This past year has been great for us – sales are up thanks to a number of new customers. Most of them were referred to us by our good friends and customers, like you, and for this we are deeply grateful.

We wish you every success in the New Year.
Sincerely,

Andrea Lawson
President

38   DO DIRECT MAIL!

Direct mail can be the cornerstone of your promotional marketing program. It needs to be done on a regular basis and is not a job for someone who does it only when they "get around to it" – you need a dedicated marketing assistant. This person can be full-time or part-time, perhaps just a few hours per week. Initially the focus should be on organizing the direct mail program – making sure that all marketing correspondence gets out on time and that the required follow-up, including phone calls, is done on a timely basis. Some firms have employed students and interns to do this, which may be a cost-effective option for your company.

Make sure you use good quality letterhead – the direct mail piece you send may be the recipient's first impression of you.

Sometimes the most challenging part of doing direct mail is developing a compelling mail piece. Here is a 10-point format for a good letter:

1. Name and Address
2. Salutation
3. Headline
4. Opening Paragraph
5. Who We Are and What We Do
6. Call to Action
7. Freebies
8. Signatures
9. P.S.
10. Inserts

1. **Name and Address**. If possible, print the complete name and address of the recipient on both the letter and the envelope. Recipients <u>will</u> read their own name and address and, if they are correct, are more likely to read the rest of the letter. There may be occasions, however, when this will be impractical.

2. **Salutation.** On routine direct mail campaigns using a mailing list, you use the standard salutation,

    "Dear Mr. _____." "Dear Ms._____ ," or *"Dear Mr. and Mrs. _____."* When you are doing more customized mailings, let's say to the members of your local Chamber of Commerce or social club, or to a group of customers, you will want to use their first names. Even though their given names may be Richard or Pamela, they may well go by Rick or Pam, and it's important to get this right. An assistant can do phone verification to get this information and then capture it in your contact management system.

3. **Headline.** Start your direct mail piece with a <u>bold headline</u> that grabs the reader's attention. If you don't get the reader's attention immediately, the letter will be in the wastebasket. The purpose of the headline is to get the reader to read the rest of the letter.

4. **Opening Paragraph**. The opening paragraph explains and expands on the headline. It must be compelling enough to keep the reader interested. It takes the reader from the headline into the declarative paragraph. It is often referred to as the "bridge."

5. **Who We Are and What We Do**. By now the reader is wondering what this letter is about, who you are and what you want. Having built up interest, you now make a strong declarative statement about who you are and what you do. For example, "We're your cost-effective alternative to the big chains!"

6. **Call to Action**. Now that you've built the reader's interest, explain precisely what you want the person to do, such as:
    - Call me today
    - Return the prepaid postcard
    - Fill out the on-line questionnaire

- Come to our open house

7. **Freebies.** This is the most important part of your letter. You must make them "an offer they can't refuse," known as a "freebie" – something the reader perceives to be of value, something they want and something they can get for free.

Here are some examples:
- Free "How to Do It Kit"
- Free product demonstration
- Free pocket guide
- Free 60-minute consultation
- Free operations review
- Coupon for $100 off on a particular product or service
- Free hardcover book
- Sample of work plan
- An offer to visit their home
- Free financial planning review

The "freebie" concept can be applied to other areas of marketing, such as an open house. Imagine how powerful it is when you say, "Come to our open house and receive a complimentary copy of our new software."

8. **Signature.** Many experts recommend at least two signatures on a direct mail piece and, if possible, one male and one female.

9. **P.S.** A postscript can be a powerful tool to get the recipient to read the letter. Direct mail experts tell us that people often read the P.S. first! Use the P.S. to highlight your most powerful "freebie" or your most compelling proposition.

10. **Inserts.** More things falling out an envelope means more things to   get the reader's attention. Examples might include:

   - A promotional flyer
   - A letter opener
   - A copy of an article

   But the most important inserts are business cards – include at least two – as the recipient may well discard the letter but keep the cards. You've probably done it yourself!

Consistency and frequency are keys to success in Direct Mail. You'll get a better return on your investment by contacting 300 prospects four times than you will by sending a single piece to 1,200.

If your business is B2B, telephone follow-up to mailings is relatively straight forward.

If your business is B2C, telephone follow-up is difficult:
- Most individuals are on a "Do Not Call" list
- They are usually not home during the day
- Many people have moved to cell phone use exclusively

In short, it's usually not worth the effort. So, let's focus on telephone follow-up to prospective business customers.

Expect a response rate of less than .5% from a mailing alone. Combine it with telephone follow-up within a week, on the other hand, and your success rate may rise to 3-4%, and occasionally even higher.

Telephone follow-up needs to be done by a marketing person with enthusiasm. When recruiting your marketing person, ask specifically about his or her willingness to do telephone follow-up and telemarketing. If the response is lukewarm (e.g., "It's not my favorite thing to do, but I'll do it if it's part of the job"), he or she is unlikely to be successful at it. The most successful marketing people are those who enthusiastically "smile and dial." If your marketing person can't or won't do phone follow-up, hire someone else on a part-time basis to do it – perhaps from their home.

Making Calls

If you've done your homework and have a good mailing list, you know the specific person you want to contact. If you don't, try asking for a specific job title (e.g. Research Director). That individual may be helpful and can act as a conduit to the decision maker. If you can establish a rapport with receptionist quickly and easily – you can tell – he/she can be helpful. "I'm hoping you can help me reach the right person…"

Scripts

We have all experienced the telemarketer who reads a prepared script – it's an instant turnoff. A **simple**, **flexible**, **friendly** approach is needed. Here are some suggested phrases/questions/topics that you might adapt to your own use:

- "Good morning. This is Diana Corbett, and I'm calling from Patrick & Company, a local office supply company."
- "I recently sent you some information and I wondered if you have received it?"
- "I believe you have recently opened a new business – is that correct?"
- "Would you like to receive our monthly list of items on sale? We'll email it to you."
- "Do you mind if I ask you a few questions?"
- "Are you currently buying your office supplies locally?"
- "Are you pleased with the service you've received?"
- "Is there anything about your current supplier you're not happy with?"
- "Would you be interested in meeting with one of our representatives? / just to get acquainted / to see if we could save you money / at your offices or here, if it's more convenient for you / at no charge, of course."

Things to Stress

- Timely service
- Competitive prices
- Knowledge of their industry
- Friendly people
- Convenient location
- Initial meeting – no cost, no obligation
- Permission to stay in touch (such as via your e-newsletter)
- Complementary catalog, kit, book or white paper

Telephone Selling Tips

BE POSITIVE	Use friendly phrases – smile.
NAME MAGIC	Use people's names whenever you can.
ANNOUNCE YOURSELF	"Hello, I'd like to talk to Gary Jones. This is Diana Corbett." State the name of the person you're calling first, then give your name – this helps the receptionist.
SPEAK NATURALLY	No mumbling, no raised voice and no eating!
GET TO THE POINT	Don't let them think you are a telemarketer.
RESEARCH YOUR TARGET	Get as much information as possible about the company before you call, including the name of the decision maker and the company's business.
DON'T GIVE UP	It may take several calls to set an appointment. Use your contact management system to keep track of everything.
HAVE A REASON TO CALL	Following up on a letter. New in town. Adding to mailing list for our newsletter
GOOD TIME TO CALL	Pick a time when most people are likely to be in.
ORGANIZE YOUR CALLS	Make new calls and follow-up calls in bunches. Plan on no more than 2-3 hours of phone work in a day to avoid "burnout."

Get An Appointment!

That's your key objective …

"Is tomorrow morning convenient or would you prefer the afternoon?"

- Schedule *something*, even if it's days later.
- Follow-up with a confirmation e-mail, brochure and map (if appropriate).

If you can't get the appointment now, get permission to keep in touch, for instance, with your e-newsletter, when you are giving a speech locally, or when you have information relevant to their business.

Conclusion

Each marketing person will figure out what works best for them – it's a matter of experience and practice. It takes time to get results, but consistency is key.

40   WRITE ARTICLES

One way to gain exposure and credibility is to write an article for an industry publication.

- Make the article highly readable and full of practical tips – stay away from technical jargon (unless that's what readers crave!)
- Come up with a title that will capture people's interest. Including numbers in the title will usually do this, for example:
    - How to Shed 20 Pounds Before Summer
    - 7 Steps to Looking Your Best
    - 13 Most Common Financial Mistakes Retirees Make
    - 12 Ways to Boost Your Internet Sales
    - 5 Steps to Getting the Best Deal on a New Car
- At the bottom of the article, ask for a "footer", which identifies who you are and what you will send the reader. For example, *Janet Ramos is a well-known dietician and fitness trainer. Call 1-800-XXX-XXXX for a free copy of her new recipe book, <u>100 Ways to Eat Happy</u>.*

41   SEND PRESS RELEASES

Press releases are a fundamental part of a marketing program. They are inexpensive, take little time to prepare, and are effective when done consistently. Set up a <u>system</u> for generating press releases so that you don't "reinvent the wheel" each time something noteworthy happens.

Compile a list of media contacts likely to be interested in newsworthy items, such as product announcements and special events. This includes contacts at newspaper, radio and TV stations, magazines, and trade and industry publications. Since the media will <u>not</u> come looking for you, it's your responsibility to create a steady stream of noteworthy items – and it may take a number of press releases before one gets picked up.

Call each media contact and get the correct name, title, address, phone number and email address of the individual to whom press releases should be sent. Then send at least one press release each quarter.

<u>Tips for Preparing a Good Press Release:</u>
- Keep it short – one page is usually sufficient.
- Double space.
- **Send a digital photograph** noting what the picture is about and give names, addresses and phone number.
- Address the press release to the **name** and **title** of the appropriate person.
- Write **For Immediate Release** at the top left.
- The headline should be underlined and briefly summarize the information in the text.
- Be factual in your wording. Avoid unnecessary elaboration.
- Answer WHO – WHAT – WHEN – WHERE and WHY in the first paragraph.
- Flesh out the details in the following paragraph(s).

- Send a brochure, background on the firm or background on the subject matter in order to validate yourself, the firm and the event.
- End the press release with '###' to indicate there is nothing to follow.

If You Get A Follow Up Call:

- Return it immediately – journalists are always "on deadline" and they will use another story if you do not respond quickly.
- Immediately send additional information if it is requested.
- Ask when the piece might appear.
- There are a number of online press release outlets. An internet search will identify the most popular resources.
- Send a thank you note.

42   GIVE SPEECHES!

Public speaking is a great way to attract new customers and it's cost-effective—you connect with a large number of people at one time.

Speaking in public rates high on the fear scale for some people – so it's not for everyone! But if you stick to topics that you know a lot about and keep it simple, you will generally get a good response. Add a useful handout and you are all set. To improve your presentation skills, join Toastmasters or a similar group.

There are many organizations that invite outside speakers, including:
- Chambers of Commerce
- Adult education classes
- Service clubs (Rotary, Lions, etc.)
- Trade groups, and
- Social clubs

But don't wait for them to call you! There's usually some competition for these speaking "slots." Send letters to these organizations, and have someone follow up by phone.

Here's a letter you might send:

Dear Chairperson:

Re: Dynamite Speakers

We have 2 partners in our firm who are **dynamite** speakers – we'll be pleased to provide testimonials!

As you plan this year's program of speakers and topics, please consider us for a presentation on (insert your area of expertise).

While we would naturally like to schedule as far ahead as possible, we have on occasion stepped in at the last moment when the scheduled speaker has canceled. For example, Chris Draegert recently gave a speech to a non-profit group when the invited speaker was delayed by weather!

Please give me a call at your convenience.

Sincerely,

John

P.S. Attached are the titles of some recent presentations.

<u>Tips for Speech Titles</u>

- Make your speech title **provocative**, e.g.
  "Never Buy Another Server!" (for a speech on cloud computing)
  "What Are You Doing After Lunch?" (for a speech on long-range planning)
  "Never Pay Taxes Again!" (for a speech on estate planning)

- Include **numbers**, e.g.
  "10 Ways to..."
  "29 Best Ideas on..."
  "13 Biggest Mistakes People Make When..."

43 RUN SEMINARS AND WEBINARS

Seminars are an excellent way to attract new customers and impress existing ones. The purpose of running a seminar is to generate sufficient interest in the subject matter that participants will want a follow-up face-to-face appointment where you can provide all the answers!

Here's a checklist:
1. Choose a subject that is topical and relates directly to your audience. They will be asking "WIIFM?" ("What's in it for me?")
2. Target your audience by only inviting people you know will be interested in the subject matter.
3. Make sure you have an **experienced** public speaker who also knows the subject matter.
4. Provide a summary of the key areas you want to address in the seminar. Back up your outline with relevant examples.
5. Run the seminar at your place of business if you have appropriate facilities, otherwise hold it at a local hotel.
6. To reduce your costs and expand your target audience, consider running a joint seminar with another group.
7. Send a cover letter together with your invitation for the seminar. Include a standard response form or faxback form to make it as easy as possible for your customers/potential customers to reply. Make sure you include a map showing the location of the venue, contact details and a 'reply by' date.
8. Follow up the invitations by email and telephone in order to generate more participants. Be sure to also contact those people who have accepted, just to remind them.
9. The best time to run the seminar is in the early evening or early morning. This reduces the impact on a customer's work day.
10. The ideal length of a seminar is between 45 minutes and 1¼ hours. This gives you the opportunity to have 2 or 3 speakers.
11. At the end of the seminar, make sure you have warm food and appropriate beverages. This is the ideal opportunity to network with customers/potential customers and to get appointments.

Giving name badges to all participants, including your team, will aid this process.

12. The day after the seminar, have your marketing person follow up and ask the questions, "Did you enjoy the seminar?" and "Would you like to be invited to the next one?"

Running webinars may be a good alternative to doing seminars – after all, it cuts the costs dramatically and therefore you can afford to do them more often. They will also help you to reach a wider audience.

44   PARTICIPATE IN TRADE ASSOCIATIONS

Join organizations whose meetings you enjoy (or you will find reasons not to participate), and then get actively involved. Volunteer for projects that have high visibility within the organization, and treat volunteer positions as you would any other professional obligation.

Here are some specific steps to take with your own trade association and with the organizations your customers belong to:

1.   Read the Association's magazines
2.   Call the editors and pitch article ideas
3.   Write and submit articles
4.   Distribute reprints of any articles you write to your entire database
5.   Write letters to the editors
6.   Join their online forums and answer questions
7.   Provide comments on their blogs
8.   Go to meetings and conferences
9.   Get on a committee
10. Volunteer to speak (or find a speaker)

45   DO TRADE SHOWS

Trade shows provide an opportunity to present and demonstrate your products and services to prospects and other "industry influentials." They provide a vehicle for getting widespread exposure and direct feedback on how your products and services are perceived. Send invitations to prospects within the geographic area of the show and take advantage of all the free publicity.

The cost of making in-person sales calls has increased dramatically over the years, and it may take five to seven sales calls to close a sale. Closing a qualified trade show prospect is often much less expensive.

Action Items

- Determine the best shows to attend in the coming year and get prior year attendance numbers and pricing.
- Investigate whether you can get "speaking slots" at the events.
- Review the activities that typically take place at a particular show and determine how to attract people to your booth.
- Make sure you're able to sell and take orders on the spot.

Here's a budget checklist for trade shows:

1.	Booth rental	$_____
2.	Banners and displays	$_____
3.	Freight	$_____
4.	Booth set up	$_____
5.	Electrical connections	$_____
6.	Tables/chairs	$_____
7.	Cleaning	$_____
8.	Giveaways	$_____
9.	Entertainment/refreshments	$_____
10.	Hospitality suite	$_____
11.	Airfares	$_____
12.	Hotels	$_____
13.	Meals	$_____
14.	Local transportation	$_____
15.	Miscellaneous expenses	$_____
	Total	$_____

Other than seminars and webinars, an "Open House" is the most frequent event that companies organize. Invitations go out to customers, prospects and referral sources. This brings a mixed group of business people to your offices. Part of the appeal will be for them to meet each other and network.

You may want to make your open house a charity fundraiser. This polishes your public image and opens up another area of contacts. If you host the event and invite your customers, the charity would likely invite their donor list (in fact, you should insist on it) – this would give you yet another group of prospective customers.

TIPS for a great Open House:

Arrange something that will be truly memorable. Here are examples:

- A raffle for something really desirable
- Long-stem roses – one for each guest to take home
- Magician, caricaturist, or other "performer"
- Live music
- **No** speeches – at least not about business
- Have a theme such as Oktoberfest

If your office or place of business is **not** conducive to hosting an open house, arrange for an unusual location, such as:

- Your local garden center – after hours, of course, with a short talk by a master gardener. Did you know that gardening is America's #1 hobby?
- Your local golf club – with a group lesson by a golf professional – this is far less expensive than organizing a golf tournament.
- A wine tasting at a winery, wine shop or restaurant.
- Attendance at a sporting event with transportation to and from the venue.

2 Ways to Celebrate Birthdays

1. Invite everyone with their birthday in a particular month to a "birthday lunch" – this works particularly well if you have older/retired customers

2. Instead of sending someone a birthday card, how about a birthday cake? Yes, it costs a little more, but consider the impact.

47   USE GIFTS, GIMMICKS AND GIVEAWAYS

People love gifts, gimmicks and giveaways – introduce a new item at least every twelve months. Here are a few suggestions:

Scratch pads	Candy
Post-it notes	Private label
Pens/Pencils	- Wine
Erasers	- Beer
Letter openers	- Olive oil
Magnets	Pot holders
Calculators	Golf balls
Rulers	Golf tees
Staplers	Polo shirts
Books	Baseball hats
Paper clips	Tape measures
Mugs	Blankets
Glasses	Luggage tags

48 GO TO LUNCH

Taking customers to lunch, dinner or breakfast, or just buying them a cup of coffee, is a good way to solidify relationships and generate referrals. During mealtimes, people tend to be more relaxed and are more likely to openly discuss their issues, giving you an opportunity to propose solutions. At some point in the conversation, customers usually ask, "So, how are you doing?" or "How's business?" This is an opportunity to tell them that things are going well, that you are looking for more customers and would appreciate any introductions.

Also establish a program of regular lunches with your other referral sources and "centers of influence".

49 JOIN A BUSINESS REFERRAL GROUP

Business referral groups (also called tip clubs or leads groups) bring business people together on a regular basis, usually over breakfast or lunch, for the express purpose of generating business for each other. The best known group is Business Networking International (BNI).

Only one person from each profession or type of business is generally permitted. Each member is expected to generate a certain number of referrals each month and there's a system for "keeping score".

If you have people in your company who want to develop a personal referral network, this is a good place to start. You may need to participate in more than one group before you find the right fit.

50 ORGANIZE BUSINESS-TO-BUSINESS LUNCHES

If it's appropriate to your style of business development, consider doing business-to-business lunches.

Invite, say, 14 people to lunch, including representatives of your company. If the desired total is 15, invite 5 customers and ask each of them to bring along one guest; the remaining seats are for members of your firm. Each prospective guest is invited by telephone and email. Try to ascertain the names of all guests in advance so you can contact them directly as well.

An ideal venue for business-to-business lunches is your own conference room, if it's big enough. Otherwise arrange for a private dining room at a restaurant.

Invite an outside speaker to give a brief after-lunch talk on a topic of interest to your guests. Examples might include the local fire chief, who could discuss safety issues in the workplace; a city planner who might discuss your community's master plan; or a bank economist to discuss the economy.

Here's a suggested format:
- Start at 12 noon and end promptly at 1:30 P.M.
- Allow 15 minutes for socializing, then have lunch.
- After everyone has eaten, have your speaker address the group for no more than 10 minutes.
- After the speech, allow time for questions and answers and interaction within the group.

Business-to-business lunches are an excellent device for bringing together referral sources (particularly customers) and their business colleagues, friends, or family members. Shortly after the event, send each guest a letter thanking them for attending, and enclosing some promotional materials. Within a week, call each person who might be a prospect and arrange for a follow-up meeting.

Every company needs a "killer" website:
- To attract prospective customers and build credibility
- To enhance relationships with existing customers
- To sell additional services, and
- To attract talented team members

Here are some practical suggestions about building a website. First, start simple. Don't pay for a site that's all singing and dancing with fast-moving graphics. Start with a simple site and add other features later on. You can post hundreds of pages of articles and tips on your site to demonstrate your expertise. Make sure that key words related to your business, your services and your products – and your location – are on the home page.

A sound investment is some form of Search Engine Optimization (SEO) which makes sure that, when someone is looking for your products or services, you appear high in the listings – like on Page 1!

Try this: Google "your profession/type of business and your city" and see where your company appears. If you're not in the top 5, it's unlikely people will find you, let alone contact you. SEO is complex and constantly shifting – most companies outsource the task to an expert.

One key component of your website is testimonials – other people saying you're "great." This will carry much more weight than anything you can ever say about yourself.

Another key component is your USP (Unique Selling Proposition) i.e. what makes you **different**. Once people land on your website, they have to find it compelling. You don't want to be perceived as "just another lawyer/veterinarian/retailer/or whatever" – you need to be different.

Here are some common differentiators:
- Unique product line/range
- Specialization in an industry/niche market
- Location
- Hours of operation
- Unique customer base
- Speed of service or delivery
- Free shipping

Any images you include on your website should be consistent with the company image you're trying to project. If you're promoting a hip and relaxed image, for example, you don't want photographs of people in suits and ties!

An interesting approach to website photographs is to have pictures of owners
- with one of their customers or
- being involved in the community.

Here are suggested features to consider for your website:
1. Home page
2. Search box
3. Useful links
4. Monthly newsletter for customers
5. Inventory of previous newsletters
6. Business articles
7. Firm profile
8. Team member page with pictures
9. Contact us page with web-based email
10. Online feedback forms
11. FAQ section
12. Daily headline news and weather
13. Map showing how to get to the office
14. Online employment opportunities page with reply form
15. Interactive calculators (for pricing, monthly payments, taxes and fees, shipping)

52   DO VIDEO!

Video is a powerful medium for generating sales. You can include comprehensive product demonstrations and user testimonials, all without having to make an in-person sales call. It can expand your market area, shorten your sales cycle, and reduce the amount of time you would otherwise have to spend face-to-face with customers.

> Make sure you avoid Helen Wilkie's "Five Deadly Website Mistakes":
> 1. Way too many words
> 2. Focus on **you** instead of **them**
> 3. Difficult navigation
> 4. No way to capture contact information
> 5. No visual interest

Include video clips on your website, and if you're blogging, do it with video. Youtube.com is one of the largest search engines, so create your own YouTube channel.

53   USE SOCIAL MEDIA!

Social networking uses the internet to maximize contact with your current network and helps you expand that network exponentially.

LinkedIn
LinkedIn allows you to link to other professionals in your industry and community. Look for "contacts" and "connections."

Facebook
Facebook is more social than professional. It allows you to connect with "friends" or become "fans" of businesses/identities.

Twitter
Twitter provides online news and views in 140 characters or less. The goal is to develop a dialogue with other users. Due to the limit on the number of characters, an entirely new language has been born. Develop "followers" and find people to "follow."

How to apply social media to your business:

LinkedIn
1. Branding for you and your company (Free profiles)
2. Business development
3. Recruitment
   - Make connections through your contacts and potentially generate business for you or your customers
   - Use the platform to research prospective customers
   - Identify ideal job candidates reviewing their online resumes
   - Use targeted advertising. For example, target LinkedIn members who are business owners and managers, in the San Francisco Bay Area, with 50-100 employees in the medical instrument field
   - Join groups and build communities with fellow professionals and companies

Facebook
1. Branding for you and your business (Free profiles)
2. Recruitment
    - Make connections with others who become friends and fans
    - Share specific information with specific "groups" of your friends
    - Recruit individuals and stay in contact with former employees
3. Build your online community of "fans"

Twitter
1. Branding
2. News delivery and receipt
3. Opinion delivery and receipt
    - Share what's on your mind with your followers and find out the thoughts of the people you are following
    - "Retweet" interesting items to followers

Tips to maximize the results of social networking:
- Educate instead of promote. People will switch off to your message if you do not add value.
- Connect your current customers with each other to help them develop new business. LinkedIn is perfect for this.
- Be regular and consistent with your communication. All sites have "feeds," and you need to be regular with your updates to make sure you are included in your network feeds. Example: Set a goal for a weekly update, and if there's no news, provide a popular quote for the week.
- Create a firm wide policy. Set the expectations for your company. Who can use the sites? How are they to be used?
- Don't expect the phone to ring as soon as you create your profile. You need to engage with your community by, for example, commenting on other people's posts. To increase visibility, be a regular contributor to other tweets, blog posts and LinkedIn/Facebook updates.

Here are some activities particularly suited to social networking:

- Recruiting – For internal and external jobs
- Engaging – For improving relationships with current customers and targeting new customers
- Educating – For demonstrating specific skills, talents and expertise
- Observing – For monitoring public comments and opinions about your business
- Social media sites are constantly changing – keep up to date with the latest trends by subscribing to blogs.

54 WOW YOUR CUSTOMERS!

A "WOW" is when a customer says not just "thank you," but "you were fantastic!"

Good service isn't enough anymore – you need to "WOW" your customers.

For example, if you don't have a particular product in stock, offer to find it, get it and deliver it, even if you have to buy it from a competitor! This type of "WOW" service wins customers for life. If you track the lifetime value of a good customer, you will find that this kind of extra effort almost always pays off.

Before you put this book away, develop a "WOW" process for your company.

Here's an example from a professional services firm:
1. Each new (prospective) customer is emailed directions to the office.
2. An assistant calls to confirm the time and location of the meeting and to find out what the customer likes to drink (during office hours!).
3. A space is assigned in the parking lot and a sandwich board says "**Reserved for Mandy Maxwell**".
4. When Mandy Maxwell arrives, the receptionist stands up, greets her by name and shakes hands.
5. The plasma screen in the conference room (or reception area) says, "**Welcome Mandy Maxwell**".
6. The receptionist already knows what Mandy likes to drink, so doesn't need to ask.
7. The receptionist asks Mandy for a business card to update the database. When Mandy leaves, the receptionist returns her business card, now laminated into a luggage tag (with your logo on the back).

If you're in retail or wholesale, set up a system to call your existing customers about new merchandise or products. Nordstrom, the department store, is an exponent of the technique.

> *"Hi Andrea, this is Sue Kingsmith at the Portland store. We have just received a shipment of beautiful shoes from Brazil. We have several pairs in your size and they are a really good buy. Please stop by when you get a chance."*

What would it take for your customers and prospects to say **"WOW"**?

55 WRITE AN ACTION PLAN!

Here are 6 steps to implementing the ideas in this book:

1. Select 6-10 ideas that suit your business and your customers, and your style of doing business.
2. Write up an action plan – we call it that because it's big on action. For each initiative, write down:
   - Who's going to do it?
   - When is it to be done by?
   - What's the approved budget?
   - What other resources are needed?
3. Monitor progress on a regular basis. Create mini-milestones to stay on track.
4. Get everyone involved and reward people for results.
5. Celebrate your accomplishments with all of your team members.
6. Repeat the successful ideas and experiment with new ones.

56   GET CLOSE WITH YOUR ADVISOR TEAM!

Work closely with your advisors, particularly your lawyers and accountants. Make sure you have a strong relationship with each of them:

- Do I like them?
- Do I trust them?
- Are they good listeners?
- Are they helping me build my business?
- Are they accessible?
- Are they proactive?
- Am I getting value?
- Do they do things on time?

H.M. Williams has written an excellent book about growing a business. It's titled <u>Proper Coffee & Other Ways to Grow Your Business</u>, published by Lawpack Publishing Ltd. and available on Amazon. He makes a compelling analogy between owning a business and owning an elephant.

Here's an excerpt:

Phase 1
You buy a baby elephant. You are bigger than it is, can see a great future with it and foresee no problems. The only concern is that you don't have any skills in managing elephants – but you think that this won't matter and off you go.

Phase 2
The elephant soon grows much bigger than you. You are no longer strong enough to control it and it takes over your whole life. It pulls you along, wreaking destruction in its wake. Standing behind it, it blocks your whole vision and you can neither see nor know where you are going. You are so preoccupied by being dragged along by it that you think there is no way to ever bring it under control. It is ruining you and your quality of life. Does this sound familiar?

Phase 3
You are one of the rare ones who decides to take advice on how to become a pukka elephant handler or *mahout*. You realize that in order to control your elephant, it is no use walking behind it ineffectually holding onto the reins as it pulls you along. You accept that you have to take a wholly different approach and that you have to learn how to manage your elephant to get the most out of it. To do this, you have to know how to sit on top of your elephant, where you can not only see where you are going, but also, with just a gentle touch with your feet on its ears, steer the elephant in the direction you want it to go. In a short time you are now running the elephant instead of it running you. As a result of accepting that you needed help, and as a result of taking professional advice, it is soon fulfilling your original dreams.

Phase 4

Once you have learned how to control your elephant, and it won't take long, you can hire and train your own *mahout* to manage the elephant for you, while you ride in the canopied *howdah* behind, sitting back and enjoying the view.